# DIVIDING THE MARITAL HOME, RETIREMENT ASSETS, & DEBTS

## Understanding the Issues, the Options, and the Consequences

ALLISON QUATTROCCHI
DIVORCE MEDIATOR, ATTORNEY

## PREFACE

Most people going through a divorce are overwhelmed by the process and the issues. Many books on divorce are available, but they are often wordy, too inclusive, and too overwhelming for a person struggling with the emotional ramifications of a divorce. This series of booklets gives the reader the ability to choose the information he or she needs and to get valuable knowledge on that subject in a quick and easy manner. The understanding and awareness these booklets can bring to the divorcing individual will contribute to that individual's ability to better manage his or her divorce. These booklets are a real bonus for the divorcing public and for professionals who work with divorcing clients.

## ACKNOWLEDGMENTS

To the many people who have contributed their knowledge, support, and encouragement to this project, and to those who have written or are writing for this project, I offer my heartfelt thanks. Special thanks to Sheila Steinberg, my editor, without whom this series of booklets would have been almost impossible.

*– Allison Quattrocchi, J.D.*
*Family Mediation Center Publishing Co.,LLC*
*Author and Publisher*

# CONTENTS

## INTRODUCTION

The two most important assets to be divided in a divorce are usually the marital home and retirement assets. Most couples also have debts, which, unfortunately, in many cases, often exceed assets. This booklet explores the various emotional and practical issues that arise around the division of the marital home, retirement assets, and debts. Although most states divide marital assets and debts more or less equally, the laws and their application vary in different states. State laws may also differ regarding the way sole and separate property* is defined and/or factored into a property division in a divorce. In any state, you and your spouse have the right to make any agreement you want regarding the division of your property and debts, but it is best to do so only after being informed about the law in your state.

The information and suggestions discussed in this booklet will make it easier for you and your spouse to make the best possible decisions around the division of the marital home, retirement assets, and debts. The more knowledge you and your spouse have in common, the more empowered you and your spouse will be to make your own agreements and/or to guide your respective attorneys or your mediator in helping you reach a mutually beneficial settlement.

---

*In Arizona, "sole and separate property" is defined as property that a spouse brings to the marriage or property that is gifted to or inherited by a spouse during the marriage. In a community property state, the law generally does not divide sole and separate property in a divorce unless it has been mixed beyond recognition with community property. "Community property" is property that is acquired by income earned from work effort during the marriage.

***What do you need to know about the division of the marital home, retirement assets, and debts that will help you and your spouse settle these issues in the most mutually beneficial way?***

## I: THE MARITAL HOME

### • Can You Keep It?

Both financial and emotional concerns need to be looked at closely before a decision is made to keep the marital home after the divorce. Following is a discussion of those concerns:

*1. Financial Concerns*

**The Increase in Living Costs for Two Households:** If viewed only from a financial perspective, divorce seldom makes good sense. Among other things, you and your spouse are probably going to double your combined housing overhead; increase your cost of groceries, household supplies, housing maintenance; incur the cost of separate health insurance for the spouse who was a dependent on the family policy; and, if there are children, increase their costs for housing, transportation, clothing, and entertainment in two homes.

The first strategy in planning for divorce and these increased expenses is for you and your spouse to look at your respective budgets. You each might begin by doing a spreadsheet on the family expenses for at least the past six months to use as a basis for projecting your individual needs for the year following the divorce. You may want to specifically research the cost of other housing options, including utilities, and what the cost of health insurance and car insurance will be under your new circumstances. Use a good monthly budget form so items are not overlooked. (One is provided in the back of this booklet.) If you and your spouse have been living separately for some time, you probably will have a better understanding of your individual budget needs than those not yet living separately.

If you have children and know how much time they will spend with you, estimate their monthly costs along with yours. If certain costs, like child care, are variable, then calculate the annual amount and divide by twelve so you have the monthly figure. If you do not yet know how much time the children will spend with you, use a separate column to estimate the cost of their needs by category for the entire month. You can adjust those costs later when you have decided how much time the children will spend with you and then add those costs to your individual monthly needs. It is important for you to get a sense of what your, your spouse's, and your children's reasonable monthly needs are for the year after the divorce, so you can answer the following question: **Is there enough money for one of us to keep the marital home at its current cost?**

At this time, look only at the overall financial picture. Child support, spousal maintenance, and the division of assets, or exploring ways to increase income or reduce expenses, will all have an impact on your ability to maintain the marital home, but it is too soon to address these issues. If there is enough monthly cash flow to keep the house, then you can start discussing whether one or both of you will own it, and begin sorting out the child support, spousal maintenance, division of other assets, and debts to test that financial feasibility more specifically.

**The Desire to Protect the Investment in the Marital Home:** Another financial consideration concerning the marital home may be the current and future housing market. If the housing market is currently appreciating and you anticipate that a good return on the investment in the home will be available to you in the future, it may be harder to consider giving up that growth by selling the home now, even when there does not appear to be enough cash flow to support the home.

The worst situation is to find that, due to market conditions (or because the home was purchased recently), you will owe money if you sell it. This, too, creates pressure to find a way to hang on to the home after the divorce, since there may not be any other resource for a down payment on another home.

The financial repercussions of keeping the home or of taking a loss as a result of selling it must be weighed carefully. The questions you might want to ask are: What kind of financial stress will result by keeping the home? What will alternative housing cost? How stable is the housing market? What is the anticipated amount of the loss, if any?

*2. Emotional Concerns*

**The Effect of Selling the Marital Home on the Children:** Most experts agree that the fewer changes you impose on children at the time of divorce the better. The same school district, the same friends, the same home may be your preferred goals in order to protect the stability of your children. Maintaining the status quo for the children may mean that one parent has to be willing to live in a much lesser residence to accommodate this goal financially.

If the goal of keeping the marital home is not attainable or acceptable as a result of the sacrifices that you or your spouse may have to make or of cash flow in general, remember that most children will adapt if your attitudes and those of your spouse are positive. Sometimes the ages of the children will determine how easily they accept those changes. Teenagers are often more upset by changes to their environment than younger children. Developmentally, they are trying to spread their wings and become less dependent on the family. Their school, friends, activities, and status are usually more critical concerns for them than for younger children. Moving may mean giving up those vital connections. The loss of the marital home or downsizing to an apartment, condo, or townhouse are also more likely to affect a teenager's self-image than that of a younger child.

However, change is a fact of life, and the world is often not fair. **All parents can do is the best they are able to do.** In the case of divorce, this may have to be the lesson for the parents as well as the children. Once again, the attitude of each parent will affect the children's attitudes about the change.

**Your Emotional Attachment to the Marital Home:** For people who have put a lot of love into their home, it is especially heartbreaking to have to leave it. People who see their home as an extension of themselves will likely go to great lengths to keep it. The danger is they may lose sight of the emotional and financial cost of doing so.

If you are weighing the decision whether to keep your home, remember how much upkeep might be involved. After divorce, if you are the spouse who is in possession of the home, all its upkeep will be your burden. In addition, you may find yourself solely responsible for a child or children for much of the time and/or be working outside the home. If you keep the home, and discover later it is financially and/or physically impossible for you to maintain it, you will have set yourself up for a possible financial loss and more heartbreak. So before making such a decision, ask yourself, **"Am I being realistic?"**

## • What Are Your Ownership Options?

### *1. Continuing to Co-Own the Marital Home with Your Spouse*

Continuing to co-own the marital home with your spouse usually makes sense only if there is a common goal shared by you and your spouse to keep the children in the home and this is the only way that goal can be accomplished. Although co-ownership can feel reasonable to people who are getting along fairly well at the time of the divorce, several problems may emerge that make this the least attractive option:

**Lack of Cooperation When the Home is To Be Sold:** If spouses intend to co-own the home, their divorce agreement will usually have some time frame that states when the home must be listed for sale and a good faith effort made to sell it by the spouse in possession of the home. Selling the home will require the cooperation of both spouses as both should agree on a realtor, perhaps have to prepare the home for sale, and sign the escrow papers for the sale. Since the resident spouse will have exclusive occupancy of the home and property, that spouse may have an interest in staying in the home for as long as possible. This interest may conflict with the agreement made at the time of the divorce regarding the timing of the sale of the home and the desire of the nonresident spouse to receive his or her share of the equity. The resident spouse is in a position to make the home difficult to show to prospective buyers or may keep it in such a condition that it does not show well. Additionally, either spouse may refuse to sign the escrow papers. A court order may remedy this behavior if it is a violation of your divorce agreement, but few people want to have to go to court to get satisfaction.

**Other Potential Conflicts Between the Spouses Regarding the Home:** When both spouses continue to co-own the marital home, they remain financially tied together through their mutual investment in a significant asset. Because the home represents an investment for the nonresident spouse—sometimes a substantial one—that spouse might display concern about or be critical of the way the home and grounds are being maintained, since these can affect the selling price and his or her net profit at the time of sale.

On the other hand, if the costs of maintenance and/or repairs for the home are being shared, the resident spouse is in the position of having to ask for reimbursement for expenditures or to seek the nonresident spouse's permission before other than emergency repairs are made. Reimbursement can also become problematic. These issues need to be clearly addressed in your divorce agreement.

The following additional areas of potential conflict in co-ownership also should be addressed in your divorce settlement agreement:

- How are the expenses, such as mortgage, property taxes, insurance, and utilities for the marital home going to be allocated?
- How are your routine repairs and major repairs going to be defined and who is going to pay for what? Are you going to share in capital repairs, such as those to roof, plumbing, electrical, air conditioning, carpet—things that are an integral part of the house—or for all repairs, and how? Will appliances such as the refrigerator, washer, and dryer, and any other appliances that can be removed from the house, be included in your agreement to share repairs?
- How is the future equity in the marital home going to be shared? Deciding how to divide the equity from the marital home at the time of sale will probably depend on the length of time you are going to hold the home and the relative responsibilities, financial and otherwise, that each spouse has for them. At the date of divorce, you may have established the equity in the marital home that you plan to share equally and have a different agreement for the way the appreciation (or loss) is to be shared at the time of the sale.
- How are the tax deductions for mortgage interest and property taxes going to be divided? For instance, if spousal support is being paid for all or part of the mortgage to the resident spouse, this would normally be tax deductible to the nonresident spouse and taxable to the resident spouse. If the resident spouse is paying the mortgage with that money and claims the mortgage deduction, those dollars for the most part escape taxation. This is only one scenario.
- Does one spouse have the right to buy out the other in the future? If so, is there a time frame, and what formula for the buy-out can be placed in the divorce agreement? An agree-

ment that provides for one spouse buying the other spouse's interest in the marital home in the future may include language about the use of an appraisal—or the average of two appraisals, if you and your spouse cannot agree on the fair market value of the home. Will a percentage for selling costs (realtors' fees and closing costs) be deducted as part of determining equity? See discussion of selling costs on pages 9-10.

- When must the marital home be put on the market for sale? If you are going to continue to co-own the home, it is wise to include in your divorce agreement some time frame for when the home is to be put on the market for sale. A provision should also be included that addresses what will happen if one spouse does not cooperate with the sale. If the divorce agreement is clear about when the home is to be listed for sale, and one spouse is not cooperating with the sale of the home, the court can appoint someone to list and sell the home pursuant to the terms of your agreement. But, again, going to court is not an attractive alternative.

In sum, continuing to co-own the home with your spouse exposes you to possible frustration and financial risks. Few attorneys would advise staying connected in a major asset with a former spouse. However, if you wish to continue to co-own your home, be sure to include clear language in your settlement agreement regarding the terms of the co-ownership. (The author encourages you to seek professional advice regarding some of these issues as everyone's situation and the options available have many variables.)

*2. Ownership of the Marital Home by One Spouse*

If one spouse is going to take the home as his or her sole and separate property, there are three common ways to "buy-out" the other spouse:

**Cashing Out the Other Spouse:** If there is enough equity in the home, the home can be refinanced or a home equity line of credit can be taken out for the amount of money necessary to pay the other spouse for his or her share of the equity in the home. The "buying" spouse needs to make sure he or she can afford the increase in the cost of the home each month because of the added payment due to the refinance or credit line taken against the home. Of course, the "buying" spouse may have other sources of cash as well, including another family member, who may step in with a loan or take an ownership interest in the home.

**Postponing the Buy-Out with a Promissory Note:** If both spouses agree, the "buying" spouse could sign a Promissory Note to the other spouse for the amount owed. This sum would be payable at some future date or in monthly installments. Interest is often paid on the sum, as the "buying" spouse has the use of the other spouse's money for the term of the note. The amount of interest is a matter for negotiation. (If you both agree that no interest is to be paid, seek advice from an accountant, as this may create an opening for the Internal Revenue Service to impute interest on the amount paid to the spouse who is receiving the payment.) It will often depend on the goals you and your spouse have regarding the marital home and the children as to how each of these issues will be resolved. If at the time the Promissory Note becomes due, the "owing" spouse cannot satisfy the note, the marital home will probably have to be sold. Or the spouses could renegotiate the note–but do not count on that occurring. A Promissory Note is a legal document and it is usually secured with a Deed of Trust against the home. This means the home becomes security for the note, just as the home is security for a bank mortgage. If the balance is not paid when it becomes due, the spouse holding the note can foreclose just as the bank can.

**Trading Home Equity for Another Asset:** Once the equity in the marital home has been established, another asset may be used as a trade for the equity in the home. Because the home and a retirement plan are often the major assets a couple has, the equity one spouse is taking in the home is often offset with the other spouse taking the retirement plan. Both spouses need to think carefully about doing this. One is giving up liquidity by getting the cash out of the home relatively quickly and the other is giving up a very valuable future asset at retirement. Depending on your goals, however, sometimes this is the most practical choice. It may be wise for both spouses to consult a financial planner. (See booklet #7, "**Divorce and Your Money**," for a discussion of the pros and cons of this type of trade-off.)

*3. Selling the Marital Home*

You could decide to sell the marital home before or shortly after the divorce. If it is not sold by the time you sign a divorce agreement, your agreement should include provisions that assign responsibility for paying the expenses, repairs, and other costs for the period between the date of divorce and the date of sale of the home, as well as the assignment of the tax deductions.

- **Calculating the Equity in the Marital Home**

Although actual fair market value cannot be clearly established unless you have a willing buyer at a certain price, a formal appraisal is the next best way to determine value. Some couples will choose instead to get comparative sales prices, called "comps," from a realtor and use an average of those values as the fair market value. This procedure is somewhat problematic because often you do not know how the home being used as the "comp" differs from your residence.

Once you and your spouse agree on the fair market value, the amount of the loan or loans against the home is subtracted from it. Often, a reasonable percentage for selling costs is also subtracted. The present value of the equity in the home may be more reasonably defined as what would be left if the home were sold now. If selling costs are not deducted from the fair market value when defining the equity, the "buying" spouse will most likely face a financial penalty in the future when the home is sold. That may alter the financial effect of the division of assets at the time of the divorce.

Other factors also might enter into the negotiation for or against the deduction of selling costs. If, for instance, the money one spouse receives for his or her interest in the marital home is going to be put down on another home, he or she faces the "loss" of selling costs in his or her new property sometime in the future, just like the spouse who "bought" the marital home. Other considerations may include: the amount of time the "buying" spouse plans to hold the marital home, the market conditions, how badly the "buying" spouse wants the marital home, and whether the reason the "buying" spouse is keeping the martial home is because both spouses want to keep the home for the children.

Sometimes the "selling" spouse will argue that selling costs should not be subtracted from the fair market value because the "buying" spouse is receiving all the future appreciation of the home. Appreciation of the property from the date of divorce forward belongs to the owner of the property, is always speculative, and is subject to the owner spouse making payments and maintaining the property. In the author's opinion, future appreciation should not be connected to the issue of selling costs.

Some courts subtract selling costs and others do not. It is another point to negotiate. If you cannot agree on your own standard of fairness, check the norm in the court where you live.

The sale of most homes today is not subject to capital gains taxes. If such taxes are relevant, this might be another offset to the equity. This discussion is beyond the scope of this booklet. (See booklet #11, "**Divorce and Taxes**," for more information on capital gains taxes.)

- **Transferring Title to the Marital Home**

Title to the marital home can be transferred by a Quitclaim or Warranty Deed. Transferring title, however, does not remove the "selling" spouse from the mortgage. Although in most states, the mortgage company cannot seek compensation from the signers on the mortgage for the home (they just take the house), credit problems can result for the "selling" spouse if timely mortgage payments are not made. If at all possible, it is wise to make every effort to refinance the home so the "selling" spouse is no longer a party to the mortgage. (See booklet #10, "**Purchasing or Refinancing Your Home**," for a complete discussion of this issue.)

## II: THE RETIREMENT ASSETS

- **Dividing Retirement Accounts**

Most retirement accounts are funded with before-tax dollars. This means that the money used to fund the retirement account has been deducted from income and no taxes have been paid on that money. Uncle Sam will get his tax dollars in the future when the dollars invested and the growth on those dollars are withdrawn from the retirement account. Assets, other than most retirement accounts, are paid for with dollars on which taxes have either been paid or are due for the year the dollars were earned. Most attorneys would recommend that, if possible, you divide the before-tax assets separately from after-tax assets, as the value of the dollar in each has a different impact. In other words, it is preferable not to offset the value of retirement assets with the equity in the car or home, for example.

To divide before-tax retirement assets, you can consider dividing each retirement asset in half or equalizing them by transferring a lump sum amount from one or more such retirement assets to the other spouse. Preferably the amount transferred should be prorated from each asset in the account. (Such a transfer will not have tax consequences as long as it is transferred between retirement accounts.) Sometimes this is not possible, is awkward, or does not meet your goals. In that event, a before-tax retirement asset must be offset with an after-tax asset and the potential future taxes on the retirement asset may affect how the retirement asset is valued.

**Do you offset for future taxes when valuing the retirement asset or assets?** Spouses and attorneys may legitimately differ regarding the fairness of offsetting for future taxes when valuing the retirement asset or assets. One approach is to reduce the value of the retirement asset or assets by some estimate of the future tax consequences. This approach has its problems.

Although taxes will eventually be paid on these assets, calculating that amount today is usually highly speculative unless the spouse who will be drawing on the fund is very close to retirement or retired. Estimating tax consequences on future dollars when they are withdrawn is usually guessing about what the future income of the person receiving the payouts or annuity will be at the time of the withdrawals and what the future tax rates will be.

Another view is that invested before-tax retirement dollars have an added value because, unlike invested after-tax dollar assets, taxes do not have to be paid on the investment return on those dollars until they are withdrawn. Those dollars then become part of the principal in the account and compound in value over the years as they also accrue an investment return. The potential for this compounding is an argument often made against offsetting the value of the retirement account for future tax liability. The net result of this view is the use of the face value of the account in the division.

The fact that determining the value of before-tax assets may be a source of conflict is another reason for keeping the division of before-tax retirement assets separate from the division of after-tax assets, if possible. If you cannot do this, it would be wise to seek the advice of a financial planner or attorney. (Some financial planners also have training as certified divorce financial planners [CDFA].)

## • Types of Retirement Assets

### *1. Individual Retirement Account (IRAs)*

All IRAs, except Roth IRAs, are funded with before-tax dollars and are always in one spouse's name. That spouse is referred to here, for discussion purposes, as the "owner spouse." This does not mean the money in that account is the owner spouse's sole and separate property. In states governed by community property laws such as Arizona and California, those funds legally belong to both spouses if the money has been earned during the marriage. Most other states will also divide those assets equally. (It is important to check the law in your state.)

An IRA can be divided with no tax consequences as long as you do not take the money out of the account in cash. Once the financial officer of the institution that holds the IRA has been presented with an order of the court (your Decree of Dissolution signed by a judge), the amount of money or percentage of assets that the decree indicates is to be transferred to the nonowner spouse can be placed into an IRA in the nonowner spouse's name with no tax consequences. In general, if the money is not placed into an IRA and, instead, is withdrawn, the amount withdrawn will be subject to income taxes and, most likely, a ten percent (10%) penalty, depending on the age of the person withdrawing the money.

If money has been withdrawn from an IRA before the divorce is final or before it has been divided or transferred to the other spouse pursuant to your divorce agreement, the IRS will look to the "owner spouse" for the tax liability on that money. It is important, therefore, to include a provision in your divorce agreement that assigns the responsibility for the taxes resulting from the withdrawal of money from the IRA. Be aware that your agreement does not bind the IRS, which can still look to the "owner spouse" for the taxes if the spouse who is supposed to pay all or a portion of them does not pay. The divorce agreement only gives the "injured" spouse the right to recover any monies that spouse had to pay to protect his or her credit from the spouse who did not meet his or her obligation for the taxes.

There is an additional type of IRA offered by employers called a Simplified Employee Pension Plan (SEP IRA). It functions exactly like a regular IRA so the same information applies to the SEP IRA as well.

Roth IRAs are funded with after-tax dollars. These dollars are different from dollars in other after-tax assets such as the home or car because the investment return on the Roth IRA dollars is not taxable when cashed out if the dollars have been in the Roth IRA for five years. Therefore, the benefit of investment return and the growth of that return over the years produces a tax-free benefit as long as you withdraw it after a minimum of five years. Roth IRAs can be divided just like regular IRAs.

*2. Employee Retirement Plans*

Most employee retirement plans are governed by federal law. (The law is known by its acronym, ERISA, which means Employee Retirement Income Security Act of 1974.) These plans usually fall into one of two types—defined contribution plans or defined benefit plans. In some cases, a retirement plan is a combination of both types of plans. These can be divided only through the use of a special court order delivered to the plan administrator. This order is known as a Qualified Domestic Relations Order (QDRO-pronounced "Qwadro"). Each type of plan is discussed below:

**Profit Sharing or Savings Plans (Defined Contribution Plans)**: Profit-sharing plans, or savings plans, are types of defined contribution plans, the most common of which is a 401(k) plan. These types of plans are funded by contributions from the employee that are tied to a percentage of the employee's earnings and are usually deducted from the employee's paycheck. The employer also contributes a percentage to the account based on the amount the employee is contributing. The value of these plans is the amount in the account. Sometimes, however, the employer's portion of the contribution plan vests to the employee by a certain percentage each year and the account may not be fully vested at the time of the divorce. The dollar amount that is "vested" is the amount the employee is entitled to at the present time. The portion that is not vested can be accessed only after a certain period of continuing employment and is forfeited if the employment is terminated. A discussion of vesting and how to treat the unvested portion of an account in a divorce is beyond the scope of this booklet. The author strongly recommends that you seek legal advice regarding the treatment of the unvested portion of any retirement plan in a divorce.

Because the dollars placed in these defined contribution accounts are before-tax dollars, the value of an account can be subject to the same arguments about value as discussed on pages 12-13 regarding IRAs. Again, it is better to divide these contribution plans by rolling over the amount for the other spouse into a separate retirement account for that spouse or to offset the appropriate sum with like-kind assets. A transfer of assets from a defined contribution plan must be made in accordance with the instructions set forth in the QDRO and the plan's policies.

In most cases, all or a portion of this sum can also be cashed out of the plan. The cash, however, can only be paid to the nonemployee spouse. Any cash distribution will incur tax consequences to the nonemployee spouse but will not be subject to the ten percent penalty, unlike cashing out an IRA. This option may provide a couple burdened with many debts the opportunity to pay off their debts from this retirement money with less of a tax penalty than if they were to use money from an IRA. Using retirement money to pay debts is not ideal, but may be reasonable under certain circumstances, and provide much needed relief. (Note: a loan may be available from the plan for you to use to pay debts as well.)

**Defined Benefit Pension Plans:** Defined Benefit Pension Plans are totally funded by the employer. The employee does not make any contribution to the plan or have a separate account in his or her name. Instead, there is a large general fund for all employees. When an employee retires or leaves the company and reaches retirement age, a calculation is made based upon a formula set out in the plan that determines the amount of the employee's monthly benefit. There are basically two ways to divide a defined benefit plan in a divorce:

- You can hire an actuary* to calculate the present value of the plan. "Present value" is an estimate of the amount of money needed in a fund today to pay the monthly benefit to the employee at retirement age if the employee left his or her employment at the time of the divorce. The amount of the benefit is based on the plan formula. The present value can then be offset in the division of marital property.
- You can choose to wait and have the benefit divided at the time the employee spouse retires and the benefit is in pay status. In many cases, the nonemployee spouse can begin receiving his or her share at the time the employee reaches the age of retirement even if the employee is still working. This division can only be implemented by entering a QDRO with the court and delivering it to the plan.

Unless the benefit is currently in pay status, most attorneys would recommend offsetting a defined benefit plan with another asset, if possible. Dividing this asset at the time of the marital dissolution makes it a cleaner division than if you wait until some future date. It also avoids you and your spouse being tied together for years to come. There are, however, other pros and cons to consider. Is the pension plan adequately funded? This has been an issue in recent years with several companies and may give each spouse pause. The employee spouse might be hesitant to pay out the other spouse's share with other assets if there are any concerns about whether the pension will be there in the

---

*An actuary is a person who computes premium rates, dividends, risks, etcetera, according to statistical probabilities, especially having to do with retirement plans.

future. The nonemployee spouse, given the same concerns, would like to have the money immediately. "A bird in the hand is worth two in the bush," as the common saying goes.

On the other hand, it rarely feels good to the employee spouse to see his or her monthly benefit reduced after retirement by the amount paid to his or her former spouse. This is a time when he or she may need the benefit the most. There are lots of factors to weigh in making this decision, including the ages of you and your spouse, how far away the employee is from retirement, the terms and policies of the retirement plan, and what happens to the plan benefit upon your death or that of your spouse. Once again, the author recommends that you discuss the options for dividing this type of retirement plan with legal counsel and/or a financial planner.

## III. THE DIVISION OF DEBT

### • Secured Assets

*1. Assigning the Debt Against the Asset to the Owner of the Asset*

A "secured asset" is one that can be repossessed if the existing debt against it is not paid. Typical secured assets are a home, cars, and other large purchases like refrigerators, washers, stereo systems, and television sets, among others. In general, most professionals who deal with divorce would recommend that if you take an asset, you also take any debt attached to it. For example, any debt against the marital home, including a credit line, should, in most cases, be paid by the spouse who is taking ownership of the marital home. By the same logic, the spouse taking ownership of a car should assume the debt that goes with the car or, likewise, the debt that is directly attached to any other property that is being assigned to that spouse. As a practical matter, this makes sense because it is very uncomfortable for the spouse who now owns the asset to have to depend on the other spouse to make payment on the debt attached to the asset. All kinds of problems can arise, including losing the asset because, unbeknownst to its owner, payments were not made.

**It is best to be in control of any debt attached to an asset you are taking out of the marriage.**

If the spouse who has the asset cannot afford the debt, rather than assigning the debt to the nonowner spouse, a better mechanism for assisting that spouse may be the payment of spousal maintenance by the nonowner spouse. Spousal maintenance can be paid to the owner spouse, who then pays the debt on that asset. Now, the owner spouse knows the bill has been paid. On the other hand, there is no guarantee that the owner spouse will pay that debt and, if the creditor can, under state law, look to both spouses for payment, a potential problem exists. The reality is that seldom does the owner of the asset want to lose the asset, so he or she is unlikely to default on the debt. The author recommends that you seek professional help if you are thinking about using spousal maintenance as a solution in this situation. There are tax implications and other legal issues associated with spousal maintenance to consider, and you may need to verify the extent of any mutual liability for a debt in your state.

If the debt is in the name of the nonowner spouse, that spouse might have concerns about what happens to his or her credit if the owner spouse does not make the appropriate payments on the debt. So, once again, there are conflicting interests between the spouses. In such a case, no agreement is going to be perfect and both spouses need to weigh the pros and cons of each option and clarify their mutual goals.

### *2. Determining the Equity of an Asset Subject to Debt*

The value of most assets is their fair market value less the debt attached to them. "Fair market value," when the property is not being sold, is the estimated amount an asset can be sold for to a willing buyer. Fair market value is not replacement value or the original cost of the asset. The amount left after subtracting the debt from the fair market value is the equity. This amount is usually credited to the spouse who is taking ownership of the asset in the division. Typically, in community property and equitable distribution states, one-half of that equity is paid to the nonowner spouse or the nonowner spouse takes ownership of an asset or assets of equal value, unless agreed otherwise.

The fair market value of real property (land and anything attached to it) may also have some amount subtracted from it to allow for the costs of its sale. This issue is discussed on pages 9-10. Capital gain taxes that are anticipated upon sale of the real property may also be deducted from the fair market value. (Depending on the size of the gain, most primary residences are not subject to capital gain taxes if the residence has been owned for two years.) The sale of stocks, and other securities, may also have capital gain consequences and cost-of-sale issues that may affect the valuing of these assets. These issues can be avoided by dividing the number of shares of stocks and other securities equally. The author is merely highlighting these issues for your awareness. Any further discussion of them is beyond the scope of this booklet.

The fair market value used for cars and similar assets is typically the trade-in value. The rationale for using trade-in value for these assets is, in general, the assumption or "best guess" that trading-in such assets is the normal way of "selling" them. Artwork, antiques, and collectibles are rather difficult to value because these assets are seldom sold directly to a buyer, but are more often sold through a gallery or auction house that takes a commission. How you want to weigh these factors in valuing your assets is up to you. If such items have significant value, it may be best to get them appraised. Be sure, however, to ask the appraiser what assumptions about the marketplace he or she is making. These assets are difficult to value. In general, if you can divide them in a way each of you agrees is fair without having to address the monetary value, it might be best to do so.

*3. What if the Debt Attached to the Asset is More Than the Worth of the Asset?*

Taking possession of an asset that has a negative value (there is more debt against the asset than the asset is worth) creates a predicament. This most often occurs with vehicles. If the asset were to be sold and debt on the asset were still to remain, both spouses may be liable for the remaining debt. Liability for this debt may be different in different states. In community property states like Arizona and California, if the debt was incurred during the marriage, the creditor can usually look to both spouses for its repayment. With some assets, usually large ticket items, the creditor can repossess the asset (cars, furniture, washer/dryers, among others) if you default on the payments. Repossession may not satisfy the debt if the value of the item is less than the amount owed. In that case, debt, for which both spouses could be liable, may still remain. Thus, it can be argued that both spouses should share in the division of the negative debt when negotiating the overall division of assets and debts.

As always, other considerations may affect your sense of fairness regarding the sharing of the debt that exceeds the value of the asset. This might depend, for instance, on which spouse is taking possession of the asset and that spouse's financial circumstances. Sometimes, one spouse takes more debt because the other spouse has no ability to pay it. A lopsided division of debt may be part of the overall approach to the amount of spousal support the spouse with the lower income will receive.

**The main point is to divide debt in a way that maximizes the possibility the debts will be paid.**

## • Creditors' Rights

**A creditor is not bound by how you decide to allocate debts in your divorce agreement. If a creditor has the ability to seek the satisfaction of a debt from both spouses either under state law, or because both spouses have signed for the debt, that creditor will continue to have the right to do so until the debt is satisfied. The term "creditor" includes credit card companies.**

For each spouse's protection, try to transfer any debt into the name of the spouse who is taking the debt. You may try asking the creditor to release the other spouse, but it is unlikely the creditor will do that. If the debt is secured with an asset, refinancing the asset is the best solution. Refinancing the asset usually needs to be done after the divorce or after marital liability is terminated (these dates may be different depending on the state) so the new debt will be free of any association with the marriage. (In Arizona, the date of service of the Petition for Dissolution terminates the community responsibility for debts incurred after that date.)

Smaller debts and credit cards for which both spouses may be liable can be transferred to a new credit card taken out in the name of the spouse who is going to be responsible for the debt. The new credit card must be taken out after the marital liability is terminated. (Be warned that in some states, such as Arizona and California, a credit card that was taken out during the marriage in one person's name does not guarantee there is no liability to the other spouse. If the card was taken out before the community has been legally terminated, the debt on that card is most likely community debt and both spouses can be held responsible for it until it is paid.) Check the law in your state.

### • Is Bankruptcy the Answer?

Bankruptcy is an extreme measure. Changes in 2005 to the federal bankruptcy law have substantially modified and, in many cases, dramatically reduced the advantages of bankruptcy. The 2005 changes are designed to benefit creditors and, in many instances, place creditors in a far more advantageous position than debtors. Seek the advice of a bankruptcy attorney before filing bankruptcy.

**Warning:** If a significant amount of debt is assigned to one or both spouses in a divorce agreement and one spouse declares bankruptcy, the other spouse may also have to declare bankruptcy, go back to court to modify the division of assets, or file a complaint to force the bankrupt spouse to pay the debts that were assigned to him or her. If bankruptcy is a possible scenario, try to divide the assets and debts in a way that avoid these kind of repercussions. Get appropriate professional assistance.

Additionally, certain assets are exempt from bankruptcy. Thus, one spouse could end up substantially better off than the other if that spouse gets his or her debts discharged and has assets that are exempt in a bankruptcy (equity in his or her residence valued up to a certain amount and retirement assets, for example), while the other spouse has the assets that are not exempt. In other words, there is a lot to consider if bankruptcy is a possibility.

In sum, there are many factors to weigh when dividing the marital home, retirement assets, and debts. If your situation is simple, this information may be all you need. If not, discuss the information relevant to your needs with an appropriate professional. Nothing in this booklet is intended to suggest how you should divide these properties or debts. The author only seeks to increase your awareness of options and consequences so you can be a more empowered client and/or participant in your divorce process.

GOOD LUCK WITH YOUR DIVORCE!

## BUDGET GUIDELINES

Budgeting is difficult for most people. Some see it as penny-pinching, others as bookkeeping. Few of us like either of these activities. Yet, budgeting is really financial planning that enables us to make intelligent decisions and rational choices.

Do not try to account for every dime as you prepare your budget. Use your checkbook records as general guidelines to fill in the categories supplied here. The purpose is to enable you to establish broad outlines, drawing on past experience, to project needs for the year following the divorce. Recognize that this budget will be different from the past.

In many marriages, one party has assumed responsibility for budgeting and handling the finances. Although one of you may be more familiar with the budget needs, each of you will probably be more knowledgeable in certain areas so don't hesitate to get some input from your spouse.

**Housing Expenses:**

If you know you are staying in the house, you will know the budget numbers. If you will be adding debt to the housing overhead because of buying the other spouse out of the house, try to estimate what this might be. If you may be in another home or an apartment or are not sure, try to estimate the cost of the alternative housing. There is space on the form for two different housing alternatives.

**Monthly Figures:**

These are monthly amounts. ANNUALIZE expenses that are not paid monthly by dividing the total amount paid annually by twelve to arrive at the figure you put on the form. Sometimes it is easier to estimate an annual amount for items such as clothing, gifts, categories under "Personal," and the like, and then divide by twelve for the monthly amount.

**Amount for Children:**

If you know the amount of time the children will be with you, you can include in your budget their costs for food, clothing, entertainment, and the like during the time they are with you. If you do not know the amount of time the children will be with you, use the separate column and estimate the total monthly figure for them. You can allocate the amount between you and the other parent as appropriate later.

JUST DO THE BEST YOU CAN. YOU MAY HAVE TO REVISIT YOUR NUMBERS AS SOLUTIONS BECOME CLEARER.

## FUTURE BUDGET

### SCHEDULE A: FIXED EXPENSES

| 1ST HOUSING OPTION | Self | Children |
|---|---|---|
| Rent or Mortgage | ______ | |
| Property Taxes | ______ | |
| Basic Telephone | ______ | ______ |
| Cellphone | ______ | ______ |
| Water | ______ | |
| Electricity | ______ | |
| Gas/Heating Oil | ______ | |
| Garbage Pick-Up | ______ | |
| Cable TV | ______ | ______ |
| Internet | ______ | ______ |
| HOA Fee | ______ | |
| Other | ______ | ______ |
| Sub Total | ______ | ______ |

| 2ND HOUSING OPTION | Self | Children |
|---|---|---|
| Rent or Mortgage | ______ | |
| Property Taxes | ______ | |
| Basic Telephone | ______ | ______ |
| Cellphone | ______ | ______ |
| Water | ______ | |
| Electricity | ______ | |
| Gas/Heating Oil | ______ | |
| Garbage Pick-Up | ______ | |
| Cable TV | ______ | ______ |
| Internet | ______ | ______ |
| HOA Fee | ______ | |
| Other | ______ | ______ |
| Sub Total | ______ | ______ |

| INSURANCE | Self | Children |
|---|---|---|
| Life | ________ | |
| Auto | ________ | ________ |
| Health | ________ | ________ |
| Fire & Theft | ________ | |
| Personal Property | ________ | |
| Renters | ________ | |
| Sub Total | ________ | ________ |

| TRANSPORTATION | | |
|---|---|---|
| Auto License Reg. (Annual) | ________ | ________ |
| Parking | ________ | ________ |
| Other | ________ | ________ |
| Sub Total | ________ | ________ |

| EDUCATION | | |
|---|---|---|
| Tuition | ________ | ________ |
| Room & Board | ________ | ________ |
| School Books & Supplies | ________ | ________ |
| Lessons | ________ | ________ |
| Other | ________ | ________ |
| Sub Total | ________ | ________ |

| MEMBERSHIPS | | |
|---|---|---|
| Union | ________ | |
| Professional Assoc. | ________ | |
| Clubs | ________ | ________ |
| Religious | ________ | ________ |
| Other | ________ | ________ |
| Sub Total | ________ | ________ |

| INSTALLMENT PAYMENTS | | |
|---|---|---|
| Auto | ________ | ________ |
| Furniture/Appliances | ________ | |

| | Self | Children |
|---|---|---|
| Charge Accounts (Accounts that have a balance to be paid off) | ______ | |
| Personal Loans | ______ | |
| Other | ______ | ______ |
| Sub Total | ______ | ______ |

**MISCELLANEOUS**

| | Self | Children |
|---|---|---|
| Anticipated Major Repairs | ______ | |
| Allowance | ______ | ______ |
| Repairs | ______ | |
| Emergency Fund | ______ | |
| Savings | ______ | ______ |
| Miscellaneous | ______ | ______ |
| Aging Parents | ______ | |
| Retirement | ______ | |
| Other | ______ | ______ |
| Sub Total | ______ | ______ |

## SCHEDULE B: FLEXIBLE EXPENSES

**FOOD**

| | Self | Children |
|---|---|---|
| Meals at Home | ______ | ______ |
| Meals Out | ______ | ______ |
| School Lunches | ______ | ______ |
| Sub Total | ______ | ______ |

**HOUSEHOLD**

| | Self | Children |
|---|---|---|
| Cleaning Supplies | ______ | |
| Repairs | ______ | |
| Yard Care | ______ | |
| House Cleaning | ______ | |
| Babysitter | ______ | |
| Day Care | | ______ |
| Other | ______ | ______ |
| Sub Total | ______ | ______ |

| **CLOTHING** | Self | Children |
|---|---|---|
| Clothes (include work clothes) | ______ | ______ |
| Laundry/Dry Cleaning | ______ | ______ |
| Sub Total | ______ | ______ |

| **TRANSPORTATION** | | |
|---|---|---|
| Gas/Oil | ______ | ______ |
| Auto Maintenance | ______ | ______ |
| Other (bus, taxi, parking, etc.) | ______ | ______ |
| Sub Total | ______ | ______ |

| **UNINSURED HEALTH** | | |
|---|---|---|
| Medical | ______ | ______ |
| Dental | ______ | ______ |
| Drugs/Medication | ______ | ______ |
| Orthodonture | ______ | ______ |
| Vision | ______ | ______ |
| Counseling | ______ | ______ |
| Sub Total | ______ | ______ |

| **PERSONAL** | | |
|---|---|---|
| Grooming Aids | ______ | ______ |
| Hair | ______ | ______ |
| Theater/Movie | ______ | ______ |
| Sports | ______ | ______ |
| Hobbies | ______ | ______ |
| Vacation | ______ | ______ |
| Newspapers | ______ | ______ |
| Magazines/Books | ______ | ______ |
| Alcohol | ______ | |
| Tobacco | ______ | |
| Home Entertainment | ______ | ______ |
| Drug Store | ______ | ______ |
| Sub Total | ______ | ______ |

| **MISCELLANEOUS** | Self | Children |
|---|---|---|
| Gifts (Birthdays, Halloween Valentine's, Christmas, Hannakah) | ________ | ________ |
| Contributions | ________ | ________ |
| Postage | ________ | ________ |
| Pets | ________ | ________ |
| Other | ________ | ________ |
| Sub Total | ________ | ________ |
| Total of Sub Totals | ________ | ________ |
| Totals from Schedule A | ________ | ________ |
| Totals | ________ | ________ |

## ANNUAL INCOME STATEMENT

| | Present<br>H | Anticipated<br>W |
|---|---|---|
| Work-related Income | ________ | ________ |
| Less Federal Taxes | ________ | ________ |
| Less State Taxes | ________ | ________ |
| Less any other deduction not accounted for in budget. | ________ | ________ |
| Net Salary | ________ | ________ |
| Interest Income | ________ | ________ |
| Dividend Income | ________ | ________ |
| Income from Trust | ________ | ________ |
| or Rentals | ________ | ________ |
| Other Income (describe): | ________ | ________ |
| ____________________ | ________ | ________ |
| ____________________ | ________ | ________ |
| ____________________ | ________ | ________ |
| Total Annual Income | ________ | ________ |
| Average Monthly Income (1/12th of annual figure) | ________ | ________ |

A list of other booklets that are available or that we will soon be publishing follows: We also intend to add others. Please check our Web site frequently for additional titles.

**www.azfamilymediationcenter.com**

OTHER HELPFUL BOOKLETS IN THIS SERIES

**#1. How to Have a Successful Divorce**
Allison Quattrocchi, Divorce Mediator/Attorney

**#2. Other Ways to Get a Divorce**
Allison Quattrocchi, Divorce Mediator/Attorney

**#3. How, What, and When to Tell the Children**
Jill Jones-Soderman, LCSW

**#4. Taking Control of Your Divorce**
Allison Quattrocchi, Divorce Mediator/Attorney

**#5. What You Need to Know About Health Insurance**
Michael J. Malasnik, Risk Specialist

**#6. Divorce and Life Insurance**
John Pope, ChFC, Life Insurance Specialist

**#7. Divorce and Your Money**
Marion Johnston, Chartered Financial Consultant

**#8. Dividing the Marital Home, Retirement Assets, & Debts**
Allison Quattrocchi, Divorce Mediator/Attorney

**#9. Divorce: Protecting Your Beneficiaries**
Thomas Murphy, Estate Planning Attorney

**#10. Purchasing or Refinancing Your Home**
Luanna Bayer, Mortgage Specialist

**#11. Divorce and Taxes**
Elizabeth Goff, CPA

**#12. How to Be a Successful Stepparent**
Joy Borum, Divorce Mediator/Attorney, and stepparent of three children

Excerpt from Booklet #1
**"How to Have a Successful Divorce"**
By Allison Quattrocchi, Divorce Mediator/Attorney

***What can you bring to your divorce so it can occur with the least amount of emotional and financial damage to you and your family?***

## I. CHANGING THE VIEW

- **The Words**

**The words you use set the stage and have the power to create the play.**

"Shame!" "Failure!" These words usually frame the initial reaction to the announcement of a divorce. Such words reflect our concerns about what our friends and family will think and the loss of hopes and dreams of what our lives were supposed to be. Cultural messages compound our sense of shame and failure. Your first positive step is to take control of that reaction and reframe it in words that are more thoughtful and caring. **Divorce is not a failure; it is a sadness.** When you change your view, you see differently.

- **Eliminating Any Need to Blame**

Viewing divorce as failure can trigger the need to blame the other person and sometimes yourself for what has happened. Blame feeds anger and creates havoc for the divorcing parties and their children. **Anger clouds judgment!** Eliminate the need to blame; it only massages your ego and creates pain. Discourage your friends and family from indulging in blame. Offer them and yourself an explanation based only on divorce as a sad reality and invite them to be supportive in a helpful way.

- **Embracing the Concept of a Successful Divorce**

**The concept of a successful divorce is as important as the concept of a successful marriage.**

Making a commitment in the beginning to the concept of a successful divorce is your choice. This choice will foster a more positive attitude, which, in turn, will improve your experience and your outcome. After all, attitude is the only thing over which you have total control. Your challenge is to move forward and not stay mired in what might have happened or should have been. No one promised you life would be fair. We all have some personal history we can choose to perceive as "unfair." It may well be unfair, but staying stuck there will only keep you stuck there. Jon Kabot-Zinn captured this concept in the title of his book, *Wherever You Go, There You Are.*

- **Taking Responsibility for Your Own Happiness**

The truth is that seldom is any one person to blame for the divorce. Usually there are several complex reasons a relationship becomes unsatisfactory. It is better to accept responsibility for your own happiness than to consume your energy in negative behavior and blaming your spouse or yourself. Easy, right? No, it is not easy. You may have to complete grieving before you can begin healing and initiating more positive responses.

In the meantime, place the following message on your bathroom mirror (refrigerator door or car visor) as a reminder, or say it to yourself every morning and as many times a day as you need in order to own it. **"My happiness depends solely on me. I alone have the power to create it."**

# Divorce Help Series

Make checks payable to FMC Publishing Co., LLC and mail to:
FMC Publishing Co., LLC • 7520 E. 2nd St., #3 • Scottsdale, AZ 85251
For faster service order online at *www.azfamilymediationcenter.com* or e-mail *sales@FMCPublish.com*.
You can also fax your order to 480-949-8814 or call us at 480-949-9511.

Print Name

Company

Address

City | State/Province | Zip/Postal Code

❑ Check/Money Order enclosed ❑ VISA ❑ Mastercard

Card Number | Expiration Date

Signature | Telephone

Please fill out the card above for address and billing information

$ ________ Subtotal

$ ________ Sales Tax*

$ ________ Shipping**

$ ________ Total (U.S.)

*Arizona residents please add 7.95% for sales tax.

** For shipping in the U.S. please add the following:

1-10 booklets add $3
11-20 booklets add $5
21-30 booklets add $7
31-40 booklets add $9

**Free shipping** on orders of 41 booklets or more

## Single Booklets • $7.95 each

- ❑ How to Have a Successful Divorce
- ❑ Other Ways to Get a Divorce
- ❑ How, What, and When to Tell the Children
- ❑ Taking Control of Your Divorce
- ❑ What You Need to Know About Health Insurance
- ❑ Divorce and Life Insurance
- ❑ Divorce and Your Money
- ❑ Dividing the Marital Home, Retirement Assets, and Debts
- ❑ Divorce: Protecting Your Beneficiaries
- ❑ Purchasing or Refinancing Your Home
- ❑ Divorce and Taxes
- ❑ How to Be a Successful Stepparent

## Package Discounts

- ❑ 11-20 Booklets . . . . . . . . . .$6.95 each
- ❑ 21-40 Booklets . . . . . . . . . .$5.95 each
- ❑ More than 40 booklets . . . $4.50 each